GORDON BARR

SURVIVAL 101

The Essential Guide to Surviving Disasters and Other Natural Disasters, Learn Everything You Need to Know On How You Can Prepare and Survive Disasters

Descrierea CIP a Bibliotecii Naţionale a României
GORDON BARR
   SURVIVAL 101. The Essential Guide to Surviving Disasters
and Other Natural Disasters, Learn Everything You Need to
Know On How You Can Prepare and Survive Disasters /
Gordon Barr. – Bucharest: Editura My Ebook, 2020
   ISBN

GORDON BARR

SURVIVAL 101

The Essential Guide to Surviving Disasters and Other Natural Disasters, Learn Everything You Need to Know On How You Can Prepare and Survive Disasters

My Ebook Publishing House
Bucharest, 2020

TABLE OF CONTENTS

WHAT IS A DISASTER?

Disasters: Why No one's Really 100% Safe

This is common knowledge - that disaster is everywhere. It's in the streets, it's inside your campuses, and it can even be found inside your home. The question is not whether we are safe (because no one is really THAT secure anymore) but whether we can do something to lessen the odds of ever becoming a victim.

First, what is a disaster, anyway? By definition, a disaster is any catastrophe or tragedy that occurs (can also be identified as a destruction or calamity). That doesn't sound good at all, does it? We should be alarmed at the mere mention of this term and we have good reasons to be because there are so many kinds of disaster.

Name it and it has it. Think of the natural disasters such as earthquakes, hurricanes, flood, tornadoes, tsunamis, cyclones, or even fire and, you wouldn't want this last one, aggression.

Accept the fact that these calamities are in all places. There are areas that are more prone to tornadoes or earthquakes and there are also some that are more exposed to cyclones.

Take a good look at San Francisco. It's a place that is literally just waiting for the next big earthquake but you can't, of course, expect the people to just leave the place and start a life some place else. Life isn't like that. In life, and in almost everything, there is always a risk. People in Sri Lanka or Indonesia should not stop living because the tsunami could strike any minute. Let's hope that point is driven.

But to better reiterate the point, let's look at a man-made disaster - aggression. Unlike the natural disasters, this is caused by people who abuse and hurt other individuals just to satiate their hunger for power, or to gain religious supremacy, or just to satisfy a craving for violence.

Whatever reasons these crazy people have in their minds, the point is, no one is safe. You could be (or so you think) locked up safe inside your home when all of a sudden someone breaks in and attacks your loved ones.

Really, no one is 100% safe anymore. You could be in the world's richest and most powerful nation or in the poorest of the poor country, still, disasters abound.

The only leverage that anyone has against disasters is preparedness. Just like an illness, it is best to prevent it from occurring instead of thinking of the many cures that could be available. Although a disaster could strike anywhere or any minute, you could, at least, perceive a disaster plan in advance.

Preparedness is compulsory to families or even individuals. Let's get down to the details.

If you're in a tornado-prone area, you should be able to set up a shelter where you and your entire family could hide when the tornado strikes.

When you're living on an earthquake belt, be sure that your home is earthquake-proof. And you should be able to immediately run under the sturdiest furniture in the house in case the roof caves in.

With people who live in areas where flashfloods occur, they should immediately renovate their home to prepare for this calamity. A few levels added to the original floor plan would be necessary. If this is not possible, then the family should be able to cooperate in saving the appliances and furniture when this destructive force of nature hits.

In the case of aggression or acts of terrorism, the keyword is vigilance. Just be alert about who you mingle with (especially when you are in a crowded area or in deserted places). Be wary of suspicious-looking people (but don't ignore the decent looking ones, too) and always be ready to act. If you can learn some form of self-defense it would be really beneficial.

In a nutshell, each individual should have a disaster plan (plan A and B, if necessary). Disasters are a reality that each of us should avoid but not ignore. Knowledge and preparedness should be able to save lives - many lives. This is not meant to frighten you but to warn you so that you could arm yourself with the essential things that you would need for survival. And the time to prepare is NOW.

CREATING A DISASTER PLAN
FOR YOUR FAMILY

What is a Disaster Plan and why each family should have one a disaster is a fact of life that no one can evade 100 percent. Calamities strike when you least expect them and they take lives by the hundreds (sometimes thousands). Although disasters can be anywhere at any given time, still, you can do something to lessen its catastrophic effects. Each family (or even individuals) should be organized and ready when the unexpected decides to show up.

Your family is the best team during disasters. First, you all know your strengths and weaknesses and you could bank on each family member's strength for the safety of your family. A family disaster plan is a MUST for every family any place in the world.

Primarily, your family should be able to point out specific disasters that are common in your area. It would be silly to prepare against tornadoes when they do not, or have never even occurred your area, in the first place. As a family, you should know what disasters usually strike in your community.

Although it's best to plan for any type of disaster, on top of the disaster plan should be your plan when the most common disaster strikes. As a family, you should be able to agree on what to do and whose role is what when the calamity happens. Each should have an equal task in countering the catastrophe.

Again, being prepared way ahead of the disaster is imperative. It is ridiculous to start talking in panic just when the family is coming face to face with, say, flood. Bear in mind the necessities that could be cut off when calamities happen: no telephone lines (or worse, no cell phone signals), no electricity, or no water. Your plan should center on establishing the most important part of survival - food and asking for assistance.

If you and your family are not confined inside your home by the disaster, it is best to go to the nearest emergency management office in your area. If you're at home and are not able to go out - don't panic. Although help could take time to arrive, most probably it will, and the best thing to do is to wait it out and have ample food while waiting for help.

Here is a simple checklist that is necessary for your family's disaster plan (but you could add more according to your family's needs):

1. Know what type of disasters plague your community and base your disaster plan on that.

2. Know if your community has a warning system. If yes, can you recognize it at any given minute?

3. Think of the people who cannot fend for themselves and who should take care of them during calamities (the elderly, disabled individuals, even pets).

4. Set a place where your entire family could meet in case your home caves in or is destroyed by a disaster. Have a plan A and plan B.

5. Have escape routes. Do not limit it to just one. Have at least two.

6. Post the emergency numbers where the flood cannot reach it and where it is safe from fire. It should be in a conspicuous area and everybody in the family should know where it is.

7. Set up a time for the entire family to practice the disaster plan at least once a month so that everyone would constantly be reminded of what they are tasked to do and how to be alert in their roles.

8. More than being physically and mentally prepared is to be prepared with necessities (food and some toiletries). Arrange a kit where there is ample food and water for everyone (at least 72 hours would be good), soap and also some spare batteries. Always include a flashlight in your disaster kit.

9. As a family, you could enroll in classes that specifically deal and discuss how to prepare your family against any disasters. A CPR or first aid class would be a necessity.

10. The last one on this list is very important: Tell your children what to expect during calamities and how not to panic. Let them know the warning signs of a potential disaster and how to contact you in case you do get separated.

Aside from all these necessary things to prepare, it is also better if you constantly keep a prayer in your heart that you and your family be kept safe from any harm during catastrophic moments.

A DISASTER KIT

The Disaster Kit: What should be in it?

Just when a disaster strikes, more often than not, families tend to panic not knowing what to do. Although, time and again, authorities tell everyone to prepare for any type of disaster in advance, many people are caught unprepared during such catastrophic events. And this is an alarming truth.

There are many ways of preparing for disasters. Your family could prepare a disaster plan where everything from escape routes and emergency communication can be discussed. The most important thing in this disaster plan should be the family's disaster kit.

By design, a disaster kit should be able to help you survive until help is at hand or until the disaster has abated. In case of floods (where you could be confined inside your home), a disaster kit should be able to provide for food and source of power while waiting for help; during earthquakes, power lines could be severed so your kit should be able to bridge those few days that you are without electricity. Your disaster kit is there for your survival.

But what's IN a disaster supplies kit? Take a pen and paper and start jotting down:

1. Keep in mind that the best time frame for any disaster kit would be AT LEAST 72 hours. So when you are planning for food that you would include in your kit, you should always multiply that by three.

2. The most basic necessities during a disaster are: water, food, supplies for first aid and sanitation, extra clothes and beddings.

3. Remember to put the necessary supplies inside an easy to carry bag (a backpack or duffle bag will do). The key here is for you to be able to get it immediately during a disaster and to carry it around with you if you have to.

4. For water: Remember to buy bottled water in advance. They are the safest and the easiest to carry. Keep in mind that different people have varying needs for water. For mothers who are still nursing their children, people who are ill or even children all have varying needs. Remember also that when the

16

weather is hot or humid, the body would need more water so better be prepared for it.

5. For food: Keep in mind that what you should bring with you are non- perishable foods. Store at least a 3-day supply of the following: canned meat or vegetables, canned soup or juices, salt, sugar, pepper (if you must), vitamins, and foods that provide energy (energy bars!). If you have kids in your family, better bring cookies and candies, too.

6. For your first aid supplies: Better bring bandages and gauze in different sizes, tweezers, scissors, wet towelletes, needle, any brand of antiseptic, thermometer, petroleum jelly, latex gloves and soap. It is also advisable to include non-prescription medicines such as aspirin, antacid, anti-diarrhea drugs and laxatives.

7. Sanitation provisions include: toilet papers, soap, garbage bags, disinfectant, chlorine and personal hygiene supplies.

8. Regarding clothing, it is necessary for each person to have at least One set of clothes and shoes (for one change). If you would need heating (and the disaster has severed that, too), then you could include a jacket and some bedding for each family member.

9. One very small but very important tool is a Swiss Army knife. This has everything that you would need during a calamity. With this, it is highly important to also bring spare batteries for your radio or TV.

Together with all the above, be sure to know some items that are not in the list but are necessary for some members of the family such as: nursing formula for infants, feeding bottles, diapers, medications, and important personal documents. For the documents, be sure that they are kept in a durable plastic envelope, plastic bag or plastic container.

These are the most basic and absolutely the most important things that you should include in your disaster kit. When you have put them all in your bag, be sure to store them in a place where you have easy access even during emergencies. Remember, be prepared in advance to lessen the panic!

HELPING YOUR CHILDREN IN A CRISES

How to Educate your Children when Crises Arise

Many disasters all over the world have taken countless lives as they ravaged on. We see the proof every day from newspapers, radio and the television. We hear of people dying because they have been unprepared when the calamity struck. And the worse thing about all this is that - the majority of the people that were helplessly killed were women and children.

Children do not have to become victims of any disaster. Even with their young minds, as parents or educators, we can help them become better prepared for any type of disaster. Just as we, adults, should be prepared to face any catastrophe, so should they. These few tips should be able to help:

1. Primarily, kids should be able to handle disasters with a sound mind and body. It is good to psychologically prepare the children of the possible disasters and the effects that they could

bring. Teach them to control fear and panic by being prepared mentally and physically. Self-confident and well-prepared kids are better able to survive disasters than weaklings.

2. If you are not contented with just you to educate your children about the effects of disasters, then you could ask for professional help. There are certain groups such as The American Red Cross that hold classes for school children. We can help our kids become ready for anything by educating them of the disasters that could happen within your community. Is your area more prone to tornadoes? Then discuss with them how a tornado develops and how they can counter its effects.

3. Discuss any disaster plan that your family has made with the children.

They should know all escape routes that the family has established (there should be at least two) and they should be able to locate these places easily. Make sure that you do not keep changing the routes. Be consistent. For much younger children (toddlers and infants), someone should be tasked to take care of them whenever the unexpected happens. This someone should be the one person that spends the most time with the younger children. For children who are already attending school, you should be able to discuss with them the routes that you have agreed upon and practice this with them (do drills) every month if you could. Doing the drills monthly would make your kids constantly aware and alert.

4. Regarding the children's disaster kits, it is highly important that you consider the age of the child that you are in charge of. If these are older children who are already attending school, then you should be able to put up a kit that includes food, bottled water (kids normally require more water than adults) and a first aid kit. Be sure they know how to use the items inside the first aid kit as this will assure their survival during emergencies when you are absent. For infants and toddlers, think of their immediate needs like infant formula, diapers and bottles. An extra blanket is also necessary for younger kids. Even though these might not be necessary for adults, children could do better with hard candies, cookies and other foods that would keep them busy or pacify them.

5. Discuss the community warning signals with your children. They should be able to recognize the warnings once they hear or see them.

6. Get in touch with the authorities in your child's school and discuss with them (in the child's presence) the disaster plan that they have. Make sure, though, that your child is able to recognize which disaster plan is for your family and which is for the school.

7. If your family has a sufficient number of adults, make sure to assign a child or two to each adult. Be clear with this plan and discuss this with the kids. Each kid should know whom to go with during emergencies.

8. Always have your children pocket a contact number of any relative that they could get in touch with in case a disaster separates you from them. This should always be in their pockets.

To sum it all up, never underestimate the mind of your kids. Most kids, nowadays, are smart. Just be constant with your plans and they should be able to remember what you have taught them.

WATCH OR WARNING

Weather Watch or Warning: Which is which?

Most people would interchange the terms weather watch and weather warning - and this is with a good reason. It's because these two terms are so intertwined that their difference is sometimes overlooked. The very thin line that separates the weather watch from a weather warning is the nearness of the weather condition.

A weather watch should always come ahead of the weather warning. Bear in mind that when you encounter the word WATCH, it actually means you need to be alert for an impending weather disaster. Weather WARNING, on the other hand, simply means the weather condition that you are 'watching' is nearing or is actually happening.

Let's discuss the weather watch first. With the issuance of a weather watch, the people are advised to make the precautionary measures that would save them from the impending weather circumstance. Some of the weather conditions that could have a weather watch would be winter storms, thunderstorms, flash floods, tornadoes or even wildfires. With a weather watch, people are being sent out the precaution that the weather condition might worsen. There is no certainty in it, though, so the weather condition might or might not worsen.

Off we go to the weather warning. With a warning, it has been observed that the storm or tornado (or whatever weather condition) is very near your area and is likely to hit it. If not, the weather condition is already or actually happening in your area. With a warning, all the indications and conditions have been seen and, hence, the issuance of a weather warning.

As families or as individuals, it is always imperative to be alert at all times. Preparedness from any form of disaster should be equally observed alongside any weather watch or warning that was issued. With the issuance of a weather watch, you should be on the standby for the approaching disaster. In case a weather warning has already been issued, then it is high time to take some shelter or to move out of the area (if necessary).

Let's look at a few weather watch and warnings that are commonly issued.

Be sure to take note of the difference in each:

1. A Flood Watch - there is a possibility that waters from higher areas have gone down to lower areas or the river would overflow at any given time. There normally would be at least 6 hours to prepare for this. It is most probable that after torrential rains, the floods would follow.

2. A Flood Warning - the flood has occurred and is near or already in your area.

3. Flash Flood Watch - this is very similar with the signs of a flood watch.

4. Flash Flood Warning - this is usually issued upon the occurrence of an ice jam, when the dam has failed or when there is torrential rain.

5. Tropical Storm Watch - storm signs are up and the winds could be ranging from 39-73 miles per hour. With this, the storm is expected to hit the forewarned area within the next 6 hours.

6. Tropical Storm Warning - this is every bit like the watch except that it's due to hit the area within the next 24 hours.

7. Hurricane Watch - within 36 hours, it is possible that the winds sustained at 73 miles per hour would hit the area.

8. Hurricane Warning - the difference is, when a wind with sustained strength of 74 mph or more is due to hit the area in 24 hours or even less. With this warning (even if the winds have already died down), it is possible that because of titanic waves that this warning would remain in effect.

9. Tornado Watch - the signs of a tornado are everywhere and it is nearing the forewarned area.

10. Tornado Warning - an actual tornado has been sighted and reported.

This is also issued when the radars have indicated the appearance of a tornado.

11. Severe Thunderstorm Watch - the conditions are favorable for a thunderstorm to develop and the signs are near the area.

12. Severe Thunderstorm Warning - the thunderstorm has been reported by 'spotters' and is already within the area or very near it.

This list should have cleared the minor difference between a weather watch and a weather warning and end the confusion.

DISASTERS AND PEOPLE WITH DISABILITIES

What People With Disabilities Need To Do To Prepare For A Disaster

When disasters strike, children, seniors, and people with disabilities or are sick are the ones that suffer most because they are usually not capable of independently taking care of themselves during such incidents. The only way for people with disabilities to be able to survive during disasters, such as fire, earthquake, flooding, hurricanes, riots, avalanche, and others, is to be prepared for any eventuality. This is especially true for those who are independently living alone.

Below is a step-by-step guide that disabled people need to do to prepare themselves for calamities and other untoward incidents:

Step 1: People with disabilities, especially the ones who are living alone, need to acknowledge that they need other persons to help them in case of emergencies. There are many who have been so used to being independent that they feel confident that whatever happens, they would be able to survive even without outside help. Knowing your limitations is the first thing you need to do to prepare yourself for disasters.

Step 2: Everybody, including disabled people, must form a support system, which is composed of at least three to four persons. If you are disabled, you need to ensure that you have support systems at home, at work and at places where you often spend a lot of time. The members of your support group must be the people you trust, such as family, friends, officemates, neighbours and even authorities, such as the police.

Your support group must be the one to inform you if there are emergency evacuations or upcoming disasters. They also must be ready to go to your house, if the need arises, to see how you are, provide what you need, or check on you once in a while during the emergency. You must also teach each member of your support team how to operate the equipment you use, such as respirators, motorized wheelchairs, etc, so that they if they need to evacuate you, both of you can act nimbly and quickly. Sometimes, a few seconds could mean your life or that of your friend or family.

Step 3: Inform your local community of your condition and your needs in case of emergency. In fact, you need to have yourself registered as a person with disability so that they can inform you immediately if there are impending disasters or respond with the right equipment in case you need a medical emergency. Local authorities won't be able to help you properly if you don't tell them about your condition.

Step 4: Prepare your own disaster plan. Surf the Internet for guidelines provided for by emergency preparedness organizations like Red Cross. You can also visit your local disaster coordination unit or local Red Cross chapter so that they can help answer your questions about your disaster preparation plan.

It is also best to discuss your plan with each member of your support group.

Try making a plan with them so that they are aware of their responsibilities and they can also help you improve your plan. Once you have finished creating a plan, do not forget to give all the members of your group a copy of the plan. You also need to have a copy of your plan handy.

Your plan must include some internal arrangements on how you would be able to receive warnings, your escape routes or evacuation plans. If you have mobility problems, you need to know what to do or how to escape your building if you cannot use the elevator. If you need electrically powered equipment, such as respirator, you must have back up plans just in case there is no electricity.

If you are dependent on a guide animal, you also need to introduce the member of your support group to your pet. It would be quite difficult for people to help you in case of emergencies if your guide animal is blocking the way and threatening to attack any member of your support group.

You also need to inform your support group where they can find the key to your house or car. Better yet, give them a duplicate of your keys so that they can enter your home when need arises. Thus, it is imperative that members of your support group are people who can absolutely be trusted because you are almost entrusting them your life.

You also need to always carry with you a health card, containing important information, such as blood type, condition, medications, or allergies, which may be needed if you are rushed to a hospital. Each member of your support group must also have a copy of this.

30

Step 5. Prepare an emergency kit, which must contain food, water, medicines, clothes, oxygen, batteries for your medical devices, and provisions for your guide animal. This emergency kit must be accessible and must be regularly checked.

You are responsible for yourself, even if you have disabilities. Thus, it is imperative that you take action now in ensuring that you are prepared whenever a disaster might strike.

HOW TO CREATE A SUPPORT SYSTEM

Useful Tips On How To Create A Support Group or System

No man is an island. Everyone needs someone, especially during disasters and emergencies. Unfortunately, nowadays, even people living near each other do not care or do not have time to care. Often times, people die alone in their houses or apartments with nobody even noticing their absence.

Because of the increasingly autonomous society we are in, all of us need to create a support group or a self-help network, which we can depend on during disasters and times of emergencies. This is especially true for people living alone, seniors, disabled, and single parents, who may find it difficult to evacuate his or her children in times of crisis.

What exactly is a support network?

As the name implies, a support network is a group of three or more people who have committed to help one another in times of need, particularly during emergencies, evacuations, and man-made or natural disasters. The members of your group will be the ones to inform, call or remind you if there is any news about impending disasters. They will be the one to notice when you are missing or know about your medical history, needs, and other important things about your condition, such as allergies or disabilities. They should be the people you trust and who trust you.

A disaster or a catastrophe waits for no one; that is why, you need to act now and start creating a support group or self help network in your neighbourhood, in your office and in places that you frequent.

Here are some important tips on how you can create a support network:

Identify the places where you need a support group

Aside from your neighbourhood or home, you also need to make a support group in the place where you spend a considerable amount of time in a week. Disasters strike anywhere and anytime, so you cannot always rely on your neighbour to be there for you when you encounter an emergency in your workplace or school. This is particularly important for people who cannot independently save themselves during catastrophes.

Choose the members of your group carefully

The key to a successful support group is trust. Since you are sharing your personal information and sometimes giving access to your private abode to members of your group, you need to ascertain that all of them can be trusted. Ideal support group members are your friends, neighbours, roommates, family and co-workers.

Make a personal assessment of your strengths and weakness

Team effort is important in such a network or group. Thus, before you can form a group, you must know what you can do and what cannot do during emergencies. This is particularly true for disabled individuals. How will your support group be able to help you if you don't tell them exactly the things that you need

34

particular help with? Moreover, they must also know your capabilities so they would know how you could help them too. If you don't know how to drive, then your group should know that so when they need someone that would require driving skills, they would call on other people or other members of the group.

Make a plan as a group

When it comes to disaster planning, two heads (or more) are definitely better than one. Therefore, you need to meet as a group to discuss the things you need to do in case of fire, flooding, avalanche, emergency evacuation, terrorist attack, riots, typhoon and other disasters. You and your group could surf the Internet, buy books, or even visit emergency preparedness organizations to help you with your plan. Furthermore, it is also wise to not only have a plan A, but also plans B and C just to be on the safe side Teamwork should already be evident during the planning stage. How are you going to entrust your family or yourself to someone who doesn't want to participate in one of the most crucial stage in emergency preparedness?

It is also important that everyone in the network have all the important numbers, a copy of the plan, and even your health records or a list of your medications. For medical emergencies, it would really be advisable that the doctors or nurses immediately know your blood type, allergies, medications, etc, in case you need urgent medical attention.

Constantly inform each other of your whereabouts

If you live alone, it would be wise to tell your support group where you are going, how long is your trip, when are you expected to return, and who you are with. This is important so that they could regularly check your house, or could inform authorities if you haven't showed up for quite sometime.

WHAT IF YOU MUST EVACUATE

What If You Must Evacuate? The Importance Of Routes And Practice

Many incidents, whether caused by humans or by nature, occur in ways that evacuation may be the only way to safety. Leaving a dangerous situation or a disaster-stricken place for safer grounds has been proven to spare the lives of countless victims from ultimate demise. For many disaster coordinating organizations around the world, evacuation from situations as small as burning buildings to large threats like hurricanes, flashfloods and even terrorist attacks may be the first step to be recommended or ordered to affected population.

So what should you do in case an unfortunate event threatens your town or city and you are compelled to evacuate your area? What are the important pointers to remember to ensure that you and your family will remain to be safe in an evacuation? Here are two important steps that can increase your chances of evacuating for safer grounds.

Know Your Evacuation Route

The most important consideration for a safe and successful evacuation is to know where to run for safety. There is not much sense in having a ready bag of survival kits but not knowing where to go. In almost any evacuation, the route to safety may be the single basic information that should matter most to anyone concerned. Knowing the evacuation route cannot be overemphasized, as this is the part of the evacuation procedure on which the success of all the other steps in the process depends.

Evacuation route plans for your city or area must be placed in conspicuous locations like bulletin boards around streets, blocks, local government offices and even popular cafeterias. Information about one's present location and the directions one should take in case of evacuation must be prominently printed on the route notices. Some important reminders to add to these postings may be the meeting places and important things one can bring when emergencies requiring evacuation do exist.

Effective evacuation route notices must have more pictorial or graphical descriptions than textual ones; this ensures that the directions can be easily memorized. Route postings should be made with materials and sizes that can be easily detached from the place where they are posted and can be conveniently carried by the evacuees.

Evacuation routes must deal with primary and secondary exit routes in your city or area. It is also helpful that assembly areas per street or block must be established in the evacuation route, this will ensure that no one in the area is left out helplessly. Local authorities and your neighbourhood must ensure that any assigned exit route must be kept clear from obstacles at all times. If possible, public address systems or speakers must be installed within the evacuation routes to remind people about things vital for survival like remaining to be calm.

Practice Your Evacuation Route

Despite advanced weather warning systems, most calamities happen without warning. The fact is that disasters can rarely be predicted in advance. The one thing that can help you and the people in your area is to have a sense of familiarity with what to do and where to go in case of emergency evacuation practices.

Evacuation route plans, no matter how important they are, may be rendered useless if the steps in the plan are carried out in a fouled up manner. The trick is to make the evacuation route plan as much a part of each individual's instincts as possible. Each member of your community must be trained to prepare for evacuation emergencies. Local authorities, particularly of those areas often visited by nature's wrath, must require their constituents to undergo evacuation drills that stick to route plans.

Conducting drills pertaining to evacuation routes provides a venue for reviewing the efficiency and effectiveness of established route plans. Regular practice of the steps embedded in your local evacuation route plan will result to a more cohesive and organized manner of vacating your affected area. Practice drastically reduces panic that can easily turn an already stressful emergency situation from bad to worse.

Evacuation route drills increase self-confidence among members of the community, which in turn increases presence of mind among individuals. And presence of mind spells safety or danger in real evacuations. Ultimately, a combined evacuation route plan known to everyone in the community and regular evacuation drills based on the route plan can be the lifeline to safety.

FIRST AID FOR FIRST RESPONSE

A Guide to First Aid Courses

Emergencies happen when you least expect it. Therefore, everybody should somehow prepare ahead and equip themselves with necessary skills or training that is needed during such instances. Everyone should undergo first aid training so that they will be ready when medical emergencies arise. It is truly frustrating to be in a position where you watch the person you love wither away and do nothing about it because you don't have the slightest idea what to do.

Importance of knowing first aid

It usually takes several minutes before a person who is suffering from injuries and other medical emergencies is brought to a doctor, a clinic or a hospital. In life threatening situations, the injured or sick person usually needs immediate aid or first response aid to help him or her survive the long wait before the arrival of medical professionals. If a person is bleeding to death, a person who knows first aid can help stop the bleeding temporarily until a professional medical practitioner is available.

The number one cause of death in the US is heart attack. And the first few minutes after the person having an attack collapses are the most crucial moments that will determine if he or she will live or die. The chance of survival of those who had received defibrillation and CPR (Cardiopulmonary Resuscitation) is about fifty per cent. In life threatening situations, a person who knows first aid will know how to bring order to the situation, help prevent further damages to the inflicted person, and even provide temporary relief or treatment.

Common Types of first aid courses

Basic First Aid Course

The first thing that you will learn in a basic first aid course is emergency preparedness. You will acquire a level of confidence that will help you be in control in certain situations, such as accidents and emergencies. Moreover, you also learn how to treat minor wounds and injuries, particularly burns, bruises and abrasions. Improper first response treatment of wounds and injuries often results in serious infection; therefore, it is imperative that everyone should know how to properly handle even such minor injuries.

In a basic first aid course, you will also learn about choking procedures and poison control. You will learn the first response treatment to broken limbs and bones. Sometimes, people with broken bones get into further serious injuries because people who move them do not know how to handle such situations properly.

Basic first aid courses will also train you to assess the situation, assess the patient and his or her conditions. Usually you need to undergo basic training before you can perform CPR and other more advanced first aid treatment.

Advanced First Aid Courses

The advanced course in first aid is usually more comprehensive in scope. Such courses will now focus on more important first response treatments on life threatening situations. The primary management of head, chest, and abdominal and pelvic injuries will be taught, as well as identification and supervision of internal wounds and bleeding. More often than not, the study of how to perform CPR and EAR (expired air resuscitation) will also be taught for both child and adult.

Specialized First Aid Courses

There are many first aid courses designed for people with particular responsibilities or concern. If you are a mother or a babysitter, you may want to attend a first aid course that is specifically designed to perform first response treatment to common emergencies concerning infants and children. It is usually very hard to determine what is bothering an infant because he or she cannot talk, so a first aid course for the care of infant and children is very important, especially for first-time parents.

If you are planning to become a lifeguard, you also need to undergo a special first aid course that specifically teaches you how to handle emergency situations in pools, lakes, seas and other bodies of water.

If you are very active in sports or are involved in sport activities, you might need a special first aid course that is specifically designed to identify and manage injuries that are linked to sport activities. Most of the training will focus on handling cramps, sprains, and muscle and bone injuries.

Prevention of sports accidents may also be included in the training.

FOOD STORES

Food Stores: The First Line Of Survival

Natural calamities like hurricanes, earthquakes, and snowstorms are but a few of the major disasters that can most certainly cut anyone's access to essential necessities, particularly food. In the most trying times during and after an onslaught of natural or manmade calamities, the most important thing to have may not be your new pair of jeans or your plasma television set; but rather your stash of food at home. Food, along with water and first aid materials, is a fundamental prerequisite for any chance of survival during emergencies.

By taking the necessary steps to store food before any disaster strikes your area, you and your family will dramatically increase your odds of making it through. Even if you are living in a modern city where most people probably think that strong winds and tremors, among other things, can hardly affect your way of life, storing an emergency food supply may still be a good thing to consider. One can never tell what will happen when disasters strike, so there can be no room for complacency even in rare places where food supply may not likely be disrupted by a calamity.

The basic considerations in storing food in preparation for emergencies include the nutritive contents and the longevity of the type of food. It is always desirable to store food that will last for an extended period of time without causing food poisoning. The most common food supply that is convenient for emergencies come in the form of canned goods, vacuum- packed goodies and handy dry mixes.

Nevertheless, perishable food stored in your refrigerator is a vital addition to your emergency food supply. They may have shorter shelf life, but steps should be taken to extend their usefulness and should never be squandered carelessly. Fresh leafy vegetables, fruits, meat and poultry can last for a few weeks even in the absence of a working refrigerator in case electricity has been cut off.

As for meat, fish and poultry, if these are frozen hard, they may last for a week or two if they are kept frozen for as long as possible. At the first sign of electrical blackout in your area, you must put newspaper and other materials in your fridge as additional insulation to prevent ice crystals surrounding your frozen food from melting quickly; thereby, lengthening the frozen state and the life of your meat, fish, and poultry. If all these steps fail, the next best option is to cook and consume your frozen food immediately.

Fresh fruits and vegetables can last for days as long as flies and other parasites are kept at bay. Keep these foods covered and dry. If there is still ample time to prepare before a calamity strikes, pickling fruits and vegetables may be a good idea; pickled fruits will provide you with all the nutritional goodness of vegetables and fruits even during emergencies.

As you start to make your food cache in preparation for emergencies, you should also take into consideration the tastes and food preferences of each member of your family. As much as possible, your emergency food supply should consist of food that is familiar to you and your loved ones. Your emergency food stash does not have to be bland and displeasing, and worse, unwholesome.

A good list of food to store for emergencies includes dried fruits, meat and fish. Canned meals, soup mixes, cereals, and noodles can provide substantial sources of energy. Do not forget high-energy chocolate bars, candies, crackers and chips to keep the kids happy. And while you are building your food store, include instant coffee, juices, milk, sugar and even tea; your body will need liquids as much as solid nutrients so do not forget potable water too.

As much as possible you should try to store food rich in energy; like food laden with carbohydrates and proteins. During emergencies, your muscles will need all the fuel they can get to function properly and efficiently. Also, try to include comfort foods in your food store; this will be good for children and adults as well. In the end, food will not only benefit your body but your determination to survive as well; as food will help decrease stress and raise the hope of survival for you and your family.

WHAT ABOUT YOUR PETS IN AN EMERGENCY

Caring for the Pets During an Emergency

Accidents and disasters can happen anytime. Things can get out of hand and before you know it, you are struck with a big problem. The damages can also be very devastating. Watching the news can sometimes help when it comes to storms and hurricanes. However, no matter how much you prepare, these events can happen when you are least prepared.

This is why people are now advised to get their own insurance. This is to protect the interest of everyone in the family in case an emergency happens. However, what about the pets? You simply cannot leave your pets alone.

Thus, it is best to ensure their safety. Ordinary insurance policies will not cover the beloved pets. Our pets are also irreplaceable to us. Thus, what can you do about your pets in an emergency situation?

The Well-Being and Safety of the Pet

There are many ways by which an owner can care for his or her pet under ordinary circumstances. However, when something out of the ordinary happens, you must also make sure that you are equipped with the right extraordinary means.

Many options are made available now to pet owners. These can provide contingency plans in case of a crisis or emergency situation. These will also ensure the safety of the pet even if disaster should strike. All it takes is for you, the owner, to know the option. Here are some of the points to keep in mind.

Securing a Pet Rescue Sticker

You can get a ET rescue sticker that will alert rescue teams in case of emergency that you have one inside your premises. These stickers come in bright colors. It will also immediately indicate the kind of pet in the house. Make sure to put the sticker in a location where people can easily see it. Put it in the window, door or gate. It must be prominently seen so rescuers can immediately respond.

Tell Your Neighbours about Your Pets

It is also a good idea to inform your neighbours that you have a pet inside the house. Your next-door neighbours can give a hand in getting your beloved cat or dog out of danger in case you are not around and something happens.

Your neighbours also can take on the task of informing the rescuers about the presence of a pet inside your premises.

Inform the Management

For people who live in rented areas or apartments, it will also be helpful to inform the management of the pets you are keeping. They can easily notify you during an emergency situation through the contact information that they require.

Contact Information of the Veterinarian

It is also helpful to keep at hand the important numbers that you can contact in case something happens to your pets. The numbers of the veterinarian and animal emergency team can be very useful when the need arises.

Store Some Pet Carriers

Animals can also panic when things go out of hand. It is best to maintain the pets within your watch. Do not let them loose as much as possible or else they might just run away and encounter more danger. Make sure that you have a pet carrier or at least a collar and leash. These will help you keep your pets beside you in case of emergency.

Emergency Kit

Consider the possible medical needs that may arise when it comes to your pets. It will be very prudent to include some stuff that in your emergency kit that your pet can benefit from.

Name Tags

Pets must also wear nametags with your name and contact number in it. This is a very good way to insure that your pets can come back safely to you in case you lose hold of them.

Microchip Option

You also have the choice to have your pet undergo a procedure to attach a microchip into the body of your pet. This is also relatively inexpensive.

Animal shelters can use the microchip information so they can reunite immediately the lost pets to their owners.

These steps will definitely ensure that the safety and well-being of your pets will not be sacrificed during emergency situations. It will help you feel more at peace with the assurance that your beloved pet is at least insured in its own way.

MEDICAL EMERGENCIES

Preparing for Medical Emergencies

Preparation is the key word to ensure that you protect your interests when things go out of hand. This is the key to minimize the loss and damages that may arise in case of medical emergencies. You only need to know specifically how to prepare for such situations.

What Is an Emergency?

An emergency situation is something that happens due to an accident or because a medical need suddenly arises. For example, a vehicular collision due to negligence of the drivers can injure passengers and passersby.

There are also instances when ordinary things turn out as a big problem due to causes beyond the control of anyone. Sometimes, an experienced swimmer can be merely taking a dip on a pool and end up with cramps and drown. This is one emergency that will call for attention.

Thus, whether it is an untoward incident or a heart attack that needs to be resolved, it is a must to be prepared to face the medical emergency.

Preparing for Medical Emergencies

There are various ways by which people can be prepared for an emergency. It all depends on your initiative to make these contingency plans a possible option when the need arises. Thus, keeping the points provided here will definitely contribute to that.

1. Emergency Contact Numbers

It is always a prudent choice to have emergency contact numbers in the possession of everyone in the household wherever they go. This will insure that you are immediately notified if something comes up.

This is also especially useful to someone who has a health condition. The emergency number can include the contact number of the physician. This can help the person attending to the situation on what things to be careful with.

2. Bring a First Aid Kit

Your first aid kit serves as your reliable supply for equipment to attend to basic medical needs. This is the best way to be prepared for any medical emergency. The first aid will be the very assistance that you can give to the person who is sick or has been injured.

There are standard first aid kits that can be purchased from the market. These kits will include the basic elements needed to attend to an injury or ailment. The list includes gauze, ointment, disinfectant, medications and a compact container.

It is also possible to make the contents of your first aid kit specific to your needs or circumstance. The first aid is crucial especially when you travel. This will keep you prepared for any situation even if you are outside the house. A first aid kit in the household can be of good use when accidents happen or when disaster strikes.

For example, going outdoors can expose you to many things. It is possible to encounter situations like bee stings, snakebites or spider bites. These are situations that are not as devastating as a heart attack, but must be properly attended with the right first aid kit just the same.

3. Emergency Supplies

Aside from the first aid kit, there are also supplies that will help you stay in control during medical emergencies. These will ensure that as you address the situation, you also get to secure the professional help needed. This is true, especially in case of more serious situations like a heart attack or someone drowning.

A flashlight is one tool that will help you if an accident occurs at night. This will provide the needed lighting so you can properly proceed with the needed medical attention.

Your cellular phone or a portable radio communication will also be useful in case of medical emergencies. This will help you immediately contact the proper authorities to ask for help. Make sure you have backup for the batteries of these tools.

4. Medical Insurance

Finally, to at least cover up for any damage or loss brought about by medical emergency situations, getting a medical insurance is the key. Some situations may require serious medical attention and treatment that can cost a lot.

Getting a medical insurance will aid you in getting the proper attention in times of emergency without the worry of the huge bills that may consequently follow.

There are things that cannot be avoided like accidents and disasters. Still, you can still be in control by preparing properly when the situation and need arise. Just keep in mind the right things to do and the tools to possess to ensure that you are ready to face any medical emergency.

SAFETY PROOFING YOUR HOME

Essential Steps to Safety Proof the House

Every family needs a comfortable and safe house to live in. It can be your dream house or a simple apartment that you are renting. No matter what type of abode you may build with your family, the number one priority is to keep it secured.

Security and safety are the primary considerations to be able to live comfortably in any household. This is the only way to sleep soundly at night when you are tired from work. It pays to have a good sleep when everyone in the household retires at night.

This is also a very crucial consideration whenever you leave the premises of the house. You have to be assured enough that the contents of the house will remain intact when you return. Thus, safety-proofing your home is really a priority. This is more than just a consideration of comfort. This is for the protection and safety of your family.

Many people will first think of getting insurance, so as to protect their interests as to the contents of the house that might be lost or damaged when untoward events happen. However, before you go that far, you must lay down a good foundation. Your house can only get a good insurance policy if you are able to provide a good groundwork in the household. This means that your house is well maintained, together with being secured.

Keep in mind that insurers will look for something that is not high risk. Thus, it is very important that you ensure the safety proofing of your home on your own too.

Some Steps to Safety-Proof Your Home

You may have some good idea on how to insure the interests of the house, but you might still be clueless on the necessary steps to keep it safety-proof. If that is the case, then reading some of the tips here can help you in your endeavour. Today, there are many ways by which you can ensure that your house is safe for living. These can also help you easily get approval for insurance applications.

1. Fencing the House

Some neighbourhoods provide security systems. However, for those who cannot rely on the group effort, you might want to consider fencing your house. This will ensure that people who are not invited inside cannot easily enter. You may also put up some alarm or security system to immediately alert you whenever an intruder comes.

2. Check the Roof and the Gutters

Any household should regularly check up the gutters and the roof. These are parts of the house that primarily protect the house. Thus, you must see if there are any cracks or loose parts so you can properly address them.

They can cause leaks if not resolved right away. This will damage the materials inside. Cleaning these areas will also ensure that they are free of debris. This will eliminate the risk of hitting someone below if a debris falls.

3. Ensure Proper Wiring

Only a qualified professional must install the electrical wiring in the household. Most fires are due to faulty electrical system. Thus, taking an extra mile for this aspect will secure a safer home for you. Take the initiative also to keep from overloading the electrical outlets. Combustible items must also be kept at a safe distance from electrical tools. Appliances must also be used properly.

4. Avoid Falling Branches

Some households have gardens that grow large trees. Some of these trees can give way to falling branches that can cause damage to property. Thus, if that happens, it will be your responsibility. This can also hurt people if any accident happens. Thus, it is best to properly maintain these if you plan to grow big trees. If possible, stick to growing smaller plants.

5. Secure a Good Gas System

The gas supply in your household is also crucial for the safety of the house. Have a qualified professional check your gas system. Have the radiators, boilers and appliances checked. Be particular also with the carbon monoxide levels emitted.

These points are helpful tips to keep in mind. These will help you in safety- proofing the home. At the same time, this will give you and your family a well-deserved peace of mind.

DISASTER INSURANCE

Preparing for a Disaster with the Right Insurance

Planning things ahead of time is the best way to ensure that you execute things the way you want them to be. However, there are some things that could happen that are totally out of the ordinary. There is no way you could plan for it.

Accidents and emergency situations are some of the instances that can really surprise you. These events are out of the control of any individual. They are beyond your means and power, just like when a disaster strikes.

Still, this does not mean that you are completely helpless in such situations. You really cannot have these events booked in your schedule so you can be out of the way when such serious disasters happen. Yet, you still can prepare for it in your own way.

Getting the Right Rental or Homeowner Insurance Policy

Owning or occupying a house entails the responsibility of taking the necessary precautions to protect the property and everyone in the household. This will, of course, cost you some amount, but it will be worth the security ensured.

There are also instances when getting covered by insurance is a requirement. Some lessors or managers of apartments will require their occupants to first get policy coverage. There are various insurance policies that can be offered to you as you occupy your house or rented premises. These will cover the usual incidents and specified risks that coincide with the occupation of the property. However, these standard homeowner policies will only cover the usual incidents that go with occupying the premises. It can cover areas such as repairs, maintenance, security or damage.

Consequences of disasters are not included.

Some standard insurance policies can cover instances of flood or earthquake. However, there is no assurance that it will cover completely everything needed. The coverage also depends on the risks in your locality to such disasters. Thus rather than wish for this, it is best to take the step to get your household covered. The key to completely protect your interests at all times is to get the right kind of insurance that you can rely on in case a disaster strikes your household.

Getting a Disaster Insurance Policy Coverage

Disaster insurance will cover any disastrous event that could be very devastating to a particular locality. This covers happenings such as tornados, earthquakes, floods and hurricanes. This will answer for any damage or loss brought about by the disaster. However, these policies will not cover the extraordinary happening of disastrous events mentioned above. You really need to get an additional disaster insurance.

Getting disaster insurance can be relatively expensive. This is one reason why most people do not immediately get it despite the fact that there really is a necessity to have one. Owners of houses do not have enough motivation to get one unless they are required. They will really not choose to buy one.

They only feel the need when the disaster strikes already, but this is too late.

It is very crucial that you get to know the risks of your home. You cannot afford to gamble with the chances and sacrifice everything you invested to the household due to a misjudgement as to getting an insurance policy.

The best resort for you is to review your options when getting an insurance policy. This is to make sure that you are properly covered for any disaster that could strike. As such, the money you will allot for the insurance will be worth the sacrifice.

Risks in the Locality

You must know the risks in the vicinity of your household. For example, some places or states are at high risk during an earthquake, especially those near the fault line. If you are in such a place, then getting covered is really a must.

Review the Terms

It is also very important to carefully read the terms of the policy. Make sure that it is favourable to you or that you will be protected in the event of a disaster. You cannot afford many exempting clauses that are as good as having no insurance at all. Get to know the instances that are covered as well those that are not. This will aid you in considering the need to get another policy to cover for those not included in your first one.

Get yourself insured now. Take these notes at hand to make an informed decision and you can be less worried in case a disaster strikes.

WHAT YOU SHOULD CARRY IN YOUR CAR

What You Need to Carry in Your Car?

There are many things that could happen to us unexpectedly. As such, it is important to be always prepared. This will help you avoid being caught off- guard. You can also minimize the problems that may later on arise. You can also equip yourself with the right information on how to handle a possible situation.

One of the most prudent decisions you can make is to know what you should carry with you wherever you may be. Basically, your preparedness will depend on the conditions. You may be prepared in your house in case of fire, but do you know what you would do in case of an earthquake?

This is where proper preparations are crucial. You should be ready to face the possible consequences of the different aspects in your life. This is true, even when you will merely go out to drive your car.

What You Should Carry in Your Car?

People who own and drive a car should know the right things that they should keep in the vehicle at all times. It is not all about safe driving on your part. Most of the time, the dangers faced in the road are due to the carelessness of other drivers.

You will definitely appreciate it if you get to prepare for the possible events that could happen as you drive in your car. This will ensure your safety as much as possible, as well the welfare of your passengers.

Here are only a few helpful tips that you can keep in mind and some of the things that you should carry in your car when you travel.

1. Cellular Phone

Most everybody now owns a cellular phone already. Still, it may be useful to make sure that you have a communication device in your car. This way, you can be certain that you can easily keep in touch with the right people if something happens.

2. Tools

You should also store tools and other useful things in your car in case something happens. Your car might get broken in the middle of your driving. It is easier to remedy the problem if you have tools and spare parts in your car to respond to the situation. Keep a tool kit in your car.

You may also want to consider bringing along extra of the other things that you regularly use. An extra battery supply can help you in case your cellular phone runs out of energy supply.

3. Emergency Contact Numbers

Also keep a list of the emergency contact numbers that you can access if something happens. This way you can easily ask for help in case of a really big problem.

4. First Aid Kit

Another thing you should constantly carry in your car is a first aid kit. This should contain the basic things that you will need to use when there is an emergency situation. You may not be a medic but you can at least resolve the minor problems that could be aggravated if left unattended.

You can also keep here the medicine that you will need for your condition, especially if you will travel for quite some time. Make sure that your companions in the car know this fact. Inform them also of where you store this.

5. Sufficient Coverage

Finally, the best protection that you can carry with you anywhere is insurance with good coverage. This will answer for any liabilities that may arise from the situation. Most of these would have very restrictive coverage in property damages.

Just make sure that you get a good coverage in your insurance. This will remove the headaches on things you have to deal with. It also secures that you will not give up a good amount of your fortune in case of collision.

Knowing what you should carry in your car is a way of protecting yourself and your love ones. This allows you to prepare for things that cannot be foreseen or cannot be helped. Thus, keep in mind the points provided here and keep your family secured.

Printed by Libri Plureos GmbH in Hamburg, Germany